My Encounter with the Concept of an Afterlife (My time of Dying)

The Very Delicate Moments

Blas D Molina

This book is a mix of medical drama, personal story, and a look into the mystery of death.

Sebastian Junger, a war reporter used to danger, had his closest brush with death in the summer of 2020 at his home. After a severe abdominal pain, he was rushed to the hospital. There, he nearly died and saw a vision of his dead father comforting him. He woke up the next day to learn he had survived a ruptured aneurysm.

This event led Junger, an atheist, to explore questions about death and the afterlife scientifically, philosophically, and personally. He wanted to understand how to deal with the sudden possibility of death, the unexplained phenomena, and the emotional and spiritual impact of facing such deep questions.

"Death isn't the end of life; it's like turning off a lamp because morning has arrived. Believing in an afterlife gives us hope that there's more beyond our physical world. It encourages us to live with purpose, find deeper meaning, and accept the mystery of what comes next. Thinking about the afterlife reminds us that life is brief and part of a much larger, ongoing story."

LEARNING HOW TO DEVELOP

Communication is a two-way road. It includes significantly more than you simply talking, you should figure out how to tune in too. Even in the afterlife.

Assuming you just worth your own viewpoint and don't consider the assessments of others then you will dislike individuals in both your own and proficient lives.

Listening is a vital expertise in being not just an old buddy, great representative or great companion, yet it makes you a superior communicator since when you hear and comprehend what the other individual is talking about, then, at that point, you can answer suitably.

On the off chance that more individuals would require some investment to tune in, there would be less miscommunication issues.

Listening seems like such an essential expertise however most individuals just hear what you are talking about, they don't tune in.

We have all been at legitimate fault for hearing yet not tuning in, we block out or fantasize or just compensation a negligible part of the thoughtfulness regarding the individual talking that we want to.

We as a whole understand what it resembles to be not exactly focusing, just to begin focusing on the grounds that an inquiry was posed of us, or a reaction is required and we are lost in our own little world, found fantasizing as opposed to tuning in.

A circumstance like this main drives the other individual mad and baffled, and it ponders gravely you.

Suppose you blocked out while your manager was talking and afterward you needed to go pose inquiries later about how to do the very thing he had quite recently clarified for you, just you were not focusing.

Part of being a decent communicator is on the grounds that the other individual regards you, we addressed this in our presentation.

An effective method for gaining the appreciation of others is by paying attention to them.

At the point when you pay attention to them, then, at that point, they will be more adept to pay attention to you when you have a remark.

Their level of regard to you has the effect between whether they are paying attention to you or simply hearing you.

Not exclusively will being a superior audience assist you with acquiring regard, yet in addition it will make you a superior representative at work and a superior mate when at home.

Everyone values having someone stand by listening to them over hearing what they say.

Furthermore, you fill your heart with joy go simpler by tuning in, on the grounds that then you get a lot more data than if you tune in with a portion of an ear; you will be more useful, more proficient and better ready to impart in light of the fact that you were focusing.

Undivided attention is the term given to when you are paying attention to the next individual as well as attempting to understand the message being sent simultaneously.

It implies that you are centered around what they are talking about, yet that you are centered around the significance behind it simultaneously.

Undivided attention implies that you are centered around their correspondence, including their non-verbal communication.

You don't permit yourself to float off and on the off chance that something is said that you disagree with, you don't crash the discussion with a contention over who is correct and who is off-base.

To see completely, you should tune in.

Assuming a subject is new to you and you are experiencing difficulty following the discussion, you can subvocalize what they are expressing to assist you with tracking and it will assist you with keeping on track.

Sub vocalization is the point at which you express something to you. Many individuals do this as they read for included center the words yet you can do this while someone is talking too.

While paying attention to one individual when in a jam-packed room, block out the side discussions since listening implies that you focus on the individual you are listening as well.

Visually engage with them frequently so they realize they definitely stand out enough to be noticed.

In the event that you think of yourself as intellectually floating off, pull your attention back on the discussion. In the event that someone endeavors to intrude, except for only a short welcome, request that they hang tight, don't hinder one discussion to begin another, leaving the individual you were conversing with remaining there considering what occurred and why.

Notoriety, recollect. Focus on their non-verbal communication that can add data about their viewpoint that the words can't, people are exceptionally expressive, so focus.

Try not to interfere with essentially to pose a case, in the event that you feel like you have an opposite assessment to their perspective, hold on until it is your chance to talk.

The possibly time it is proper to hinder is the point at which you not satisfactory about something that you have quite recently said and you wish to explain it.

You can hinder to seek clarification on pressing issues, however ensure that you make sense of that you are not comprehend and that you need to, so they realize that you are intruding on justifiably.

By posing inquiries when you don't comprehend something, you are finding a way incredible ways to keep away from miscommunication sometime later.

For instance, let us say you are conversing with a business partner about something that his specialty is doing, and your manager is thinking about doing likewise for your specialization, yet you want to get some data first.

On the off chance that your partner makes sense of it yet you don't actually grasp it however don't seek clarification on pressing issues, when you give your rendition of it to your chief, it probably won't be correct.

Nonetheless, in the event that you pose inquiries until you completely comprehend, when you report to your chief, you will actually want to give him a precise portrayal.

Showing that you are listening is a piece of being an attentive person. Continuously recognize that you are tuning in as well as that you are really focusing.

You can utilize non-verbal communication to flag that you are tuning in by gesturing your head or you can basically say "uh huh" or simply make a delicate sound so they realize that you are still with them during the discussion.

They shouldn't need to figure on the off chance that you are focusing or not, your non-verbal communication, disposition and verbal pieces of information ought to be all that they require to realize that you are tuning in and focusing.

One more method for showing that you are listening is to at times reflect back what was recently expressed, like saying, "do I see accurately, you are saying."

Of simply reword information disclosed to both explain it and to ensure that you comprehended it right.

In the event that something isn't thoroughly clear, seek clarification on pressing issues, this shows that you are tuning in as well as that you have an interest in what they are talking about.

Sometimes giving an outline of what has been said back will assist with clearing up miscommunications while showing that you are tuning in.

Keep in mind, individuals value being listened as well and when you get a standing just like an extraordinary audience then it goes far to assisting you with being an incredible communicator since individuals will be more able to pay attention to you.

In the event that you disagree then express your viewpoint separately. Never start a contention.

YOUR COMPOSURE SHOULD BE POWERFUL

Prior to conveying any composed correspondence, you want to know who the crowd is with the goal that you can convey the properly organized message.

You would express an email to your companion equivalent to you would to a work partner, or possibly you shouldn't.

Do you have to send an educational email, a specialized report, or an update to a client?

Your organization and tone of your composing is something essentially vital to your correspondence.

Understand what your listeners might be thinking before you start to organize your correspondence.

Who are the interest group and what kind of message should be conveyed?

How much is a lot to say or on the other hand on the off chance that you cross the line will the real message get stalled in the tedium of it?

Assuming that you make it too short, significant data might be lost. Assuming you make it excessively specialized and send it to a not comfortable individual with the language that you utilized, the whole message won't seem OK.

You want to ship off a message, however to have it be perceived.

The objective of composing, except if you are holiday and are simply refreshing family, is to convey an idea, and generally, the faster and more clear that you can make yourself clear, the better.

In the first place, who is your crowd?

What do they definitely be aware of the subject?

On the off chance that they know about the greater part of it, and you are simply adding data, stay away from re-composing the whole thing assuming they definitely know a large portion of it.

Begin with a short synopsis of the circumstance to remind them and afterward delve into the new subtleties. On the off chance that someone is uninformed, begin toward the start.

You want to understand your listeners' perspective with the goal that you understand what sort of data to put and the amount to place in the composition.

On the off chance that you have one primary concern, make it the focal point of the composition; try not to put such a lot of additional data around it with the goal that the primary concern gets lost.

On the off chance that you are attempting to pass on a ton of data, rather than one long report, split it up into sensible segments, utilize more limited sections, list items, or even intense headings to call consideration.

On the off chance that you are composing a report of a discourse, instead of wind up meandering aimlessly and wandering out of control, begin with a blueprint.

A diagram is an extraordinary method for coordinating your considerations so you don't wind up with a report or piece of correspondence that is difficult to follow or comprehend.

Frames permit you to deal with the data so it streams better and is in more modest segments and simpler to follow.

Appeal to the close to home part of your message. In the event that you believe the beneficiary should do something specific, for example, purchase your item, help out with a school sports pledge drive, and so on. you want to give reason that inspires an emotional response from them.

Try not to just request their help or request that they purchase your item, however explain to them why too, what advantages will they get from concurring?

Remember your objective as well as the necessities of who your crowd is too.

Keep your language straightforward and straightforward. Except if you are composing something brimming with specialized language that is going to a beneficiary who will grasp it, try not to use over specialized wording.

Your perusers will lose all sense of direction in the words that they don't have the foggiest idea. Same with enormous words, you may thing that it makes you look keen to sprinkle whatever number long words as could be allowed into the correspondence yet odds are it will simply make you look self important and you will lose your crowd.

Some portion of understanding where your listeners might be coming from is understanding what they need from you.

What are they anticipating that you should give or tell them of in your message.

While communicating something specific, remain focused; you have a central matter that you are making, give your all to impart it obviously.

Your peruser doesn't have any desire to peruse a whole page just to find the one sentence that is pertinent to them.

In the event that you understand where your listeners might be coming from and you understand what they are expecting, you keep your message short and to that point.

In the event that you really want an answer from the individual, make certain to clarify what you need to be aware.

Assuming you want something from them, what do you need?

What advantage is there for them?

Continuously view at your correspondence from their side too, give them an explanation concerning why they should seriously mull over doing what you inquire.

Individuals like to know the intentions and explanations for demands. Assuming you have questions and need them to respond to it, obviously state what it is that you want replied or what you want an assessment on.

Continuously follow up. At the point when you follow up, that causes the peruser to feel like your message is significant, or that the way that they got it is significant, this causes them to feel significant.

Continuously circle back to a call, email or even a letter, simply a method for telling them that what you sent was significant.

Watch your composing design, attempt to not lump a lot of data into one segment and more terrible yet a strong page of composing.

Make your correspondence look satisfying to the eye, yet utilitarian also by utilizing headings, subheadings, passages, list items, brief numbered blueprints, and intense print.

Use headers, diagrams, graphs, and even pictures to assist with coming to your meaningful conclusion. It separates the text and gives the perusers something to check out, something to relate the data in the text to.

Continuously edit. Syntax mistakes and spelling blunders will degrade the message that you are attempting to get out and it simply looks amateurish.

Virtually all word handling projects and email programs have an underlying spell check, however there are a few things, for example, an abused word, that a spell check program won't get, so you should continuously edit the report cautiously.

A few words sound the same; ensure that you are utilizing the right word. Particularly in the event that you are not a local English speaker, you should watch out for this.

By changing your settings in your promise handling project to edit for however many things as would be prudent, you will dispose of the possibility having this occur, yet no program will at any point be comparable to your own eye.

A decent clue for editing is to begin at the lower part of the report and read towards the top, going in reverse. You are more able to get botches that way.

Particularly in the work environment, with approaching cutoff times, you can wind up sending things out hurried.

A quickly composed email or report is more inclined to having mistakes than one that you required some investment on.

Prior to conveying anything don't simply run it through a spell-check, read it yourself. Botches generally consider inadequately yourself, regardless of how much thought and exertion you put into your correspondence, the mix-up will establish a more drawn out connection than the actual message will.

TIPS IN ADVANCED COMMUNICATION

With the progression of innovation, the utilization of telephones is reducing for a more computerized age, where increasingly more correspondence is done electronically.

Gone are the times of the blaring fax machines and here are the times of messaged reports all things being equal.

Not any more trusting that the mail will bring that necessary report, it tends to be messaged and show up immediately, from anyplace on the planet.

On account of the indifferent idea of electronic correspondence, we don't necessarily in every case understand what precisely who our listeners might be thinking is, yet we understand what we want to convey.

Keep things formal and unbiased.

Regardless of whether furious, or answering something that you got that was genuinely charged, don't answer similarly.

You might reserve the privilege to feel furious, baffled, or even hurt by something that you have gotten however you ought to never allow your feelings to direct your correspondence.

You have no clue assuming that the individual you are answering to will advance what you ship off another person, which makes you looks terrible.

Keep your tone nonpartisan. Assuming you are vexed or furious over something, explain it why you are irate, keeping the correspondence affront free.

Keep away from forceful phrasing or reaction inciting hits, this is your vocation, so be proficient, regardless of whether the other individual isn't really.

In the event that the subject in question is a tricky one, you should consider having the discussion face to face or via telephone rather than through composed correspondence.

The issue with the composed word is that the other individual will in some cases read a specific tone to what you are talking about, or confuse the tone that you were going for, which will just expand the contention and drag out the issue.

Continuously read and afterward re-rehash business correspondence to ensure that you tone is nonpartisan.

This is particularly valuable assuming you are disturbed at something, or the individual that you are writing to, recollect, you need to be proficient so keep the tone and setting of your correspondence unbiased and not combustible.

In the event that you are feeling like what you composed may be excessively sincerely charged, have some time off, and return.

Ask another person to peruse it prior to sending it to ensure that you have come to your meaningful conclusion plainly and accurately and that it isn't incendiary.

A subsequent assessment is generally something worth being thankful for so when given criticism, consistently give it thought.

On the off chance that you end up playing the email label game, where you and the other individual are continually going this way and that over a similar issue and nothing is any nearer to being settled then it was a couple of hours prior, stop the cycle.

Once in a while correspondence is better when done up close and personal and this is one such circumstance. Save you, and them, a few time and handle the matter face to face either through telephone or with a short gathering, that way you can deal with the circumstance at that moment without the to and fro and sitting and hanging tight for an answer.

Keep business messages as only that, business. Practically all business correspondence should be signed in and is normally documented.

In the event that later on you want to survey the correspondence for a specific detail or snippet of data and on second thought of a couple of messages, you find a few messages, going this way and that about non-business things it will be baffling and tedious. Keep your business messages about business.

Whether you are sending an email inside, composing a note of gratitude to a client, or setting up a report, your business correspondence ought to constantly be expertly composed and thoughtful.

Regardless of whether you have a comment that you realize the other individual won't have any desire to hear, be thoughtful.

You can state things cautiously so you are not glossing over reality yet you are likewise not beating them about the head with it simultaneously.

Keep away from fault language or whatever is accusatory, for example, sentences that start with "I" or "You."

In the event that a mix-up has been made, the individual who made is possible mindful of it, accusing them won't fix the misstep nor does it advance kindness in the work place.

Keep away from negative things, consistently recast things, since no one needs to peruse an email that is all despondency or excessively basic.

In the event that you should reprimand, attempt to do as such without being critical and list the great parts alongside the terrible parts.

Never center exclusively around the negative, regardless of whether the negative could out weight the positive.

Part of being nonjudgmental is that you focus on what's relevant and keep your viewpoints out of it, except if inquired.

Pick your words cautiously while making your correspondence, an unfortunate selection of words can change the whole importance of your correspondence.

Very much like in a discussion, it isn't what is said or composed that is significant yet rather it is what the other individual receives in return.

Keep your business correspondence clear and simple to peruse. Pick a textual style that is not difficult to see and peruse, and stay away from extravagant foundations that can make the textual style hard to see.

For unadulterated comprehensibility, dark textual style against white is the least demanding to see. Keep the extravagant text styles that are difficult to peruse, shaded text styles and custom foundations for your own correspondence.

Similarly while utilizing letterhead, ensure that the shade of your paper doesn't make the textual style hard to peruse, so utilize a lighter tone so the textual style appear simpler.

The main proper time that the message ought to be fancier or message impacts utilized ought to be during introductions or publicizing flyers.

MAKING YOURSELF CLEAR

Part of being a successful communicator implies that you know how to make yourself clear thoughtfully and keeping in mind that not taking part in strategies that end up in a warmed contention.

Figuring out how to have a distinction of assessment, without cutting to the chase of contending is a compelling correspondence expertise.

Having the option to really make yourself clear is exceptionally valuable in all parts of our lives since clashes, minor and major, are a piece of life.

We end up attempting to get our side heard both at work and at home and having the option to guilefully win the discussion or contention without it getting profound on either side is a tremendous in addition to have the option to do.

Except if you can really make yourself clear, persuading others to do what you need or to consent in your mind will be essentially unthinkable.

With a couple of straightforward deceives, you can make your discussions more compelling and get individuals to see your side with considerably less quarrel.

For this segment, we will utilize the word contention, yet we mean just a conversation with different sides, not a sincerely charged contention, but rather basically where more than one individual is attempting to accomplish something out of the conversation.

While attempting to prevail upon individuals, the primary thing you should know about is your central matter.

Assuming you ramble nonsensically such a lot of that they couldn't figure out what your objective is, they will always be unable to either concur or differ assuming that they are absolutely ignorant regarding your situation or objective.

Each contention has an ideal result, so before you take part in a conversation about something, know plainly what it is that you need.

We banter a wide range of things to get something, for example, to get your kids to tidy up their room, to persuade a client that your organization will do the better work, that your thought working will be the best one to set in motion, or even to deal over a cost on a trade-in vehicle.

Prior to participating in a contention, understand what it is that you need to accomplish toward it's end.

Having a reasonable objective as a main priority will assist you with outlining your discussion in like manner. Never participate in a contention only for having a discussion or a contention.

The secret to making yourself clear is to constantly keep composed. Regardless of whether the other individual is off-base and you can demonstrate it, by getting exasperated and freaking out, you will just consider inadequately yourself and afterward your message will be eclipsed by your explosion and regardless of how organized the realities are that you needed to introduce, they will be limited as a result of the way that you introduced them.

Regardless of whether the other individual hotels to affronts, never fight back. Keep your side of the contention unbiased and try not to be wry or critical.

You need to be heard and not hindered so consistently give that equivalent civility to other individual, or people who are talking.

Hold on until they are finished talking before you offer your viewpoint on what they have recently said and avoid intruding.

Individuals value being paid attention to, so regardless of whether they like your perspective, in the event that you pay attention to them, they will pay attention to you.

On the off chance that the contention winds up getting warmed, simply leave. Nothing will be acquired by having a genuinely charged contention.

Compromise is something that you should acknowledge as a result. Not all contentions will turn out your direction, regardless of how powerful you are at conveying; a trade off is in many cases an effective method for fulfilling each of the gatherings that way everyone gets something that they needed.

Figure out how to acknowledge splits the difference.

At the point when you understand what the result is of your desired contention, you can start to valuably outline your contention.

For instance, simply advising individuals to do things a specific way won't ever work, you need to give them justifications for why they ought to.

Of assuming that you are attempting to hear individuals to help your point of view on something, you can't simply anticipate that they should concur without having some kind of data to back up why your perspective is right.

Individuals need to have confirmation, proof, and realities to back up things prior to pursuing a choice.

In the event that you were making an attempt to sell something, you wouldn't go to a client to make the pitch without having diagrams, charts, raw numbers to back you up.

Whenever you are arguing for something, you want to have an adequate number of supporting focuses to back up what you are talking about.

Particularly in the business world, in the event that you are going to a gathering or a meeting where you realize that you will wind up in a discussion over something attempt to plan ahead.

Make an agenda of your desired focuses to make and the supporting contentions for each point. Then attempt to take a gander at things from the opposite side and attempt to resolve those issues in your contention as of now.

For instance, in the event that you give a discourse and, there is a Q & A period, you can anticipate that there should be a few inquiries contradicting your perspective, so attempt to expect these and be ready for when they come up.

Continuously counter your rival's contention with statistical data points, don't simply deviate, you must be explicit about why you conflict.

What benefits does your point have over their point?

Keeping your tone impartial, you ought to continuously consistently move toward contentions to attempt to call attention to blemishes in the opposite side, as long as you have something to back up why it is imperfect.

You generally need to have data to back up your viewpoint.

Remain on moment that you are in a discussion or contention, recall you have an objective and assuming you get off point or get occupied, you will wind up not accomplishing your objective. Others will utilized interruption strategies to get you off subject, know about this, and steer the discussion back to the point within reach.

STEP BY STEP INSTRUCTIONS TO DELICATELY CONVINCE

Connected at the hip with actually making yourself clear is having the option to convince individuals to your perspective, or into aiding you.

Salesmen are astounding at influence, their responsibility is to convince you to buy something, regardless in the event that you really need it or not.

Legislators convince individuals about what they vow to do.

Kids convince guardians that they will do either in return for a specific toy.

You could convince your mate into allowing your folks to remain for a little while.

Influence is the point at which your correspondence is powerful sufficient that it impacts the other individual to pursue a choice, in support of yourself, in view of your contention.

The capacity to have the option to convince is exceptionally valuable. It will give you the edge when you want to introduce your venture at a gathering at work, to your clients, or on the other hand on the off chance that you are attempting to enroll others to help you out with something.

Anyone who has at any point needed to move realizes that the influential ability is an extremely convenient device!

An incredible method for convincing others is an extremely inconspicuous stunt, it is unobtrusive to such an extent that it really deals with an inner mind level and assists the other individual with relating to you more straightforward.

This method is called compatibility and when you ace it, it will help you while convincing individuals that you don't have the foggiest idea.

As people, we will quite often feel good around things that are natural to us, and by laying out affinity with someone, we are doing exactly that, and they will be more loose and more open with you, expanding your possibilities getting what you need.

You lay out compatibility by coordinating and reflecting the individual's non-verbal communication, discourse examples, tone, and volume and by utilizing a portion of the very expressions or words that they will generally utilize.

You should be unobtrusive about this since, supposing that you are seen it will look as though you are ridiculing the other individual and not exclusively will affinity not be laid out, however that individual's assessment of you will be negative.

Keep in mind, notoriety is something that you should know about and secure. You should stand by listening to what they say, yet additionally the way that they express it for everything to fall into place.

Keep your talking volume equivalent to their volume is. On the off chance that they increment their volume, in almost no time, you increment your volume to coordinate.

Same thing with the speed of discourse, on the off chance that they are talking at a high speed, you talk at a similar speed too.

You ought to match their tone too, in the event that they are talking in a sluggish, loosened up tone you do likewise however on the off chance that they are talking in a more energized pitch, you likewise utilize that equivalent energized tone.

At the point when your discourse designs are comparable, it causes you to appear to be more natural and dependable, and accordingly, they are more able to consent to do what you need.

On the off chance that they will generally utilize a specific word or expression frequently, utilize that state likewise, yet sparingly, so it isn't as though you are clearly replicating their utilization of the word.

In any case, by sometimes utilizing a word that they use frequently, you will lay out compatibility with them.

Non-verbal communication is significant when you are laying out affinity; attempt to reflect their non-verbal communication decently well.

Assuming that they are hanging over the table, you incline in moreover. On the off chance that they are sitting with their leg crossed, cross your leg also. In the event that they shift positions, stand by a little while and shift to a similar position, simply don't change to match their situation while they are as yet moving, that will be excessively self-evident.

On the off chance that they make a motion, attempt to make a comparable signal when you talk. Assuming you are a male verbal blistering a female and she contacts her hair, rather than that, when you talk, change your tie. You don't need to do precisely exact thing they do, yet make a comparative signal; it helps set them straight.

At times, while attempting to be convincing, only the realities that you have are sufficiently not to influence someone to your side or to inspire them to concur.

In cases like this, there are alternate ways of aiding prevail upon them to your side.

By rehearsing the accompanying, you will expand your influential abilities and will improve your probability of getting what you look for from individuals.

These strategies are particularly helpful for individuals working in deals and a large portion of these are educated at deals classes or in studios since they are exceptionally successful.

Focus on all that the other individual says or does. No one can really tell when some little detail can be utilized for your potential benefit.

At the point when we discuss advantage, we don't mean exploiting individuals.

Our procedures are generally not intended to hurt individuals, not to find a shortcoming and exploit only for individual increase.

Notoriety, recollect. These procedures are intended for you to get the high ground all good so you don't set a standing for playing messy up to get what you need.

In the event that you are experiencing difficulty making an association with the other individual, or your contention simply is staying put, recollect your discussion with them.

Have they referenced a side interest that they appreciate, a film they saw or perhaps referenced a new excursion?

Bring it up in a cordial manner, and lay out a shared conviction and afterward endeavor to convince them again about what you need.

As well as settling on something worth agreeing on, win them over, not exclusively will it help your standing, however it will help when it comes time to convince them about what you need.

Converse with them and figure out what they like and aversion and afterward accomplish something that they like as a cordial motion. Assuming you know something that disturbs them, take care to not do no matter what.

Keep your tone agreeable and never become whiny about being turned down. You will get turned down at times however in light of the fact that they turned you down around a certain something, doesn't imply that they will turn you down about different things.

Nonetheless, in the event that you have a fit at being turned down, you will make it unimaginable for yourself to at any point convince that individual later on.

Assuming you handle being turned down with effortlessness and respect, they will recall that, and could surrender later on another theme.

AVOID STAGE FREIGHT

Notwithstanding the way that certain individuals seem, by all accounts, to be awesome at public talking, most of the populace views this as extremely overwhelming and nerve-wracking.

Nonetheless, public talking, similar to all abilities, is an expertise that you can develop. Your message will be better gotten in the event that you go up there without losing your place, failing to remember your lines, or having your voice shake.

Nerves are ordinary, yet the most ideal way to counter a terrible arrangement of nerves about talking openly is by planning.

Being arranged in advance is the most ideal way to guarantee an extraordinary discourse.

Regardless on the off chance that simply a casual show at work, a show to a client or a discourse at a full meeting, you can improve as a speaker with some fundamental planning before you even open your mouth.

You can never practice enough. In the event that you are believing that you could feel like a moron in the event that someone discovers you rehearsing your discourse, simply envision the amount of a food you will seem to be on the off chance that you don't practice and you commit an error while giving the discourse before individuals.

Assuming you are apprehensive about talking openly, disregard retaining the whole discourse. Depend on elegantly composed notecards that are clear and simple to peruse for the body of your discourse.

Rather than attempting to pack full sentences onto a card, only a couple of words, similar to you would place in a framework to help you to remember what you are talking about.

Notecards are an extraordinary method for ensuring that you forget about nothing; however, ensure that you number them so you realize they are in good shape!

Do have the initial assertion and the end articulations remembered. These two sections establish the greatest connection so consistently establish a decent connection.

At the point when you are composing your discourse, consider your crowd and their assumptions as well as your desired message to get across.

Could it be said that you are showing them something, enlightening them something or convincing them regarding something?

Deliver sure that your discourse makes progress toward your objective while remembering your crowd.

What does the crowd realize about anything that you are discussing?

You should be mindful so as to not fly right by them with data and to not patronize them by the same token.

On the off chance that you are looking at something they are curious about, keep your language basic and relate the data to something that they can connect with more straightforward.

You really want to do some examination on your crowd, what are their objectives and their necessities that your discourse needs to give.

Ensure that you obviously characterize the reason for your discourse so the crowd knows right from the outset what they are there to achieve.

Would could it be that you need or need them to escape your discourse, which ought to be obviously expressed in the initial articulation and again summed up in your end explanation.

Try not to give your discourse so short that you can't cover all that you require to and don't fix things such that long that you lose your crowd's consideration.

Allude to your notes in the event that you want a little update. Ensure you cover each of the principal parts without over-burdening them on data.

Visual guides are perfect, however they ought not be the focal point of your discourse. They ought to be utilized exclusively to back up specific places or to delineate something that you are saying.

You don't have to have a visual guide for each significant point. At the point when you have such a large number of visual guides, the crowd becomes muddled in the event that they should watch the slides or paying attention to you.

At the point when you depend on visual guides, you limit your contact with the crowd. You are there to connect with them, visually engage, and make sure to grin.

At the point when you are turned around to take a gander at the visual guide despite you are showing them your good faith, this is an enormous slip-up.

Continuously continue confronting the crowd while giving your discourse, when you have a visual guide up, you ought to have a note card of what it says so you don't need to pivot.

Walking out on the crowd can break the association that you have laid out with them.

Try not to deliver your discourse excessively dry all things considered. Regardless of whether giving a discourse brimming with specialized language, you ought to pepper up the discourse with things to liven up your crowd's consideration or to hold it back from straying.

Utilizing visual guides is one method for accomplishing this, yet use them sparingly. Attempt to energize your discourse with some humor, recount to a funny story that connects with the subject in some way occasionally to hold your crowd back from losing interest.

Keep in mind, continue to visually connect with the crowd, and fight the temptation to gaze at your notes.

When you have your discourse composed and your notes and visual guides arranged roll out no improvements to the discourse.

This resembles changing your response without a second to spare on a test when your most memorable response is typically correct.

Try not to allow nerves to get the better of you and your discourse will be fine.

At the point when you continue to change things in your discourse, it is more enthusiastically for you to recollect what you have added, and what you have taken out.

Get it composed, and afterward practice, endlessly practice. Try not to change it, transform it, or modify it.

Record yourself giving your discourse, either on record or simply on a sound recorder. Play it back, observing where you really want to get to the next level. Continue rehearsing your discourse, utilizing your notes, until you feel like you know basically everything there is to know about it.

The day preceding your discourse, attempt to do things that loosen up you. On the off chance that you are good to go, focusing on as of now might be adverse to you.

Survey your discourse a couple of times, yet ensure that you get a lot of rest. Prior to falling asleep, imagine how your discourse will go the following day; see yourself giving a discourse without any blunders, no nerves, and no mix-ups.

The force of perception is serious areas of strength for exceptionally, when you go to give your discourse, require one moment to review your representation from the prior night and how it affected you, feel that equivalent inclination occasionally give your discourse, feeling the very certainty that you felt in your perception.

How would you talk while not talking out in the open?

Do you utilize signals or potentially move around somewhat?

Odds are you do. At the point when you can keep the very sort of characteristics that you ordinarily have while giving your discourse, it will assist you with being more loose and your discourse will be all the better for it.

Take a stab at unwinding and utilizing some non-verbal communication as opposed to standing frozen completely still, it will give your discourse stream better and will make it sound more normal and look less constrained.

Make sure to visually connect also. Try not to zero in on only one individual, however make a point to glance out around the group, not zeroing in on only a couple of individuals, but rather the group all in all, keep your consideration zeroed in on them while giving them your discourse.

An extraordinary method for encouraging connect with your crowd is to have an interactive discussion after you give the discourse.

This allows the crowd an opportunity to explain something they might have missed, get more data and all the more significantly, to focus closer on you and what you are talking about.

By skirting on a responsive period, you are passing up on an extraordinary chance to interface with additional individuals.

IMPROVING YOUR COMMUNICATION

Correspondence is an important expertise for our expert lives. Without it, we were unable to associate with our collaborators, our clients, or our companions.

The better your relational abilities are the better and more proficient you will be at your particular employment.

Bosses frequently effectively search out workers who have extraordinary relational abilities since they know that makes them a superior representative.

We might think we are extraordinary communicators, however actually, the majority of us are not.

We grow up learning a specific method of correspondence and that is difficult to survive.

Some of the time, even an individual with a professional education will pepper their discussion with such an excess of shoptalk that you wind up flabbergasted that they graduated secondary school, not to mention got a degree.

It isn't exactly what we say that establishes a connection with others; it is the way we express it also.

In the business world, impressions mean the world, and you should make a decent one to climb the business stepping stool.

Correspondence is in our non-verbal communication, our looks; it is with regards to what we say and our tone as well as the actual words.

You should know about how you are talking, particularly while meeting individuals interestingly.

You don't welcome business partners equivalent to you would a companion, nor would you address them the same way.

Business correspondence is in every case more formal, and ought to be kept nonpartisan in tone.

That implies you keep your non-verbal communication impartial too. In the event that you tell someone you are paying attention to them, yet it doesn't give the idea that you are, then they expect you are not.

Visually engage, gesture at times and, surprisingly, incline towards them to show that you are being mindful.

Regardless of whether they say something you disagree with, keep your face nonpartisan. Keep on an indifferent appearance since one misconstrued look that you make can have an extremely dependable terrible effect.

Business correspondence is about regard and civility, so consistently stay nonpartisan in tone, regardless of whether you need to word something unequivocally, do as such in such a way with the goal that it isn't fiery, pernicious, or annoying.

Business correspondence is generally reality based, no assessment based so except if you have realities to back up your viewpoint, avoid your perspective with regards to it except if explicitly requested it.

Try not to be critical and never make suspicions on what another person will say, do or act since that simply opens up a wide range of entryways that lead to contentions and bad sentiments all around.

Try not to fault and keep away from proclamations that tell another person how they feel, stick to how you feel and what you know, no speculating.

Business correspondence ought to be immediate and it ought to be clear. The significance of the correspondence ought to be not difficult to sort out and not lost in a ton of additional cushioning.

Individuals are occupied, so when they read an email or start a short discussion, they hope to keep it that way, short.

Yet again focus on what matters as you most likely are aware them and make your point exceptionally understood and straightforward.

Try not to make the other individual attempt to think about what the place of the discussion is.

At the point when another person is talking generally focus.

Request explanation on the off chance that you are can't say much about what they are talking about or on the other hand to ensure you comprehend them accurately.

While paying attention to someone, focus on their non-verbal communication too.

Assuming that you really want something explained, be clear about what you don't have the foggiest idea. Answering with only a "what" ponders inadequately you.

Let them know what you really want explained or which part you don't have any idea so they know what to turn out once more, or what to go over an alternate way.

Don't hesitate for even a moment to get clarification on some pressing issues however ensure they are significant ones.

We have all been in a gathering with someone who poses vast inquiries for not an obvious explanation other than to draw out the gathering.

That kind of correspondence fills compelling reason need and ought to be stayed away from.

All business correspondence has a reason, and you ought to know about that reason before you talk or write to make sure that it is understood.

Discussing clear and straightforward, ensure that you have a talking voice that is unmistakable and straightforward.

Everyone gets anxious, certain individuals are modest, yet even still, you really want to ensure that your voice is clearly sufficient to be heard.

Try not to mutter, or talk while dismissing or talk so low that even the individual close to you can't hear you.

While addressing someone, see them, don't drop your head down and gaze at your feet or the table while talking, it suppresses your voice and makes it hard to figure out you.

Ensure that when you are talking, that you are conveying your message plainly.

Is the message getting past or is the other individual looking a piece lost and confounded?

In the event that they are looking lost and confounded, have a go at making sense of an alternate way.

Hang tight for criticism or search so that clues with their non-verbal communication could check whether you are perhaps going to quick or on the other hand assuming you really want to make sense of something once more.

Abstain from being excessively easygoing while having a discussion at work.

Keep your non-verbal communication some-what formal and your tone something very similar.

Keep in mind, how you impart in your own life isn't the manner by which you ought to convey at work, particularly not if you need to go far in your vocation.

Figure out how to deal with discussions or inquiries over the thing you are proposing without freaking out. Not every person will continuously concur with something you are saying or something that you are proposing so you want to figure out how to contend for your goal handily.

Particularly while managing clients, you never blow your top and you never resort to offending the other party, your opposition or more awful, your client.

Likewise, when you are addressed, be thoughtful about replying as opposed to being irritated at the inquiries.

The place of correspondence is to convey an idea so you can't possibly be furious or baffled on the off chance that the other individual is just attempting to accurately grasp the message.

In the event that they don't comprehend a large number of you have made sense of it a couple of times, maybe you really want to change how you are making sense of it.
Activities to Further develop Correspondence

Notwithstanding the earlier sections, there are additionally a straightforward ways of cleaning up your relational abilities.

You can find out about how to improve yet except if you set out to really utilize the learning, you won't ever get to the next level.

This part manages some essential correspondence practices that you can do to work on both your verbal and your composed correspondence.

Activities to further develop verbal relational abilities

Might you at any point name a solitary day where you didn't converse with anyone, not even once?

We bet you can't. Verbal correspondence is a piece of our regular routines, which is something to be thankful for in light of the fact that it implies that rehearsing great communication is extremely simple.

Verbal correspondence is the simplest sort of correspondence to rehearse, on the grounds that you get moment input from the individual you are conversing with.

Everything thing you can manage is practice your casual conversation on others.

As you approach your day, converse with individuals as opposed to disregarding them. Make it a highlight welcome individuals, even the ones you don't have the foggiest idea and make casual banter with them.

Express welcome to individuals in the lift in the mornings and coming back. At the point when you stop to get espresso, rather than a surged "much obliged" while staying away from eye to eye connection, look at the clerk without flinching, tell them "bless your heart" with a grin, and add, "Have a decent day."

Ask the corner store chaperon how their day is going. En route to your work area, pause and make some casual banter with individuals that you work with as opposed to floating passed them unobtrusively.

At the point when you begin becoming acclimated to making casual conversation in your day to day routine, it isn't no joking matter to unexpectedly need to do it in a business setting or when at a party.

One more method for rehearsing your talking abilities is to pick a point and afterward without placing a lot of thought into it, deliver extemporaneous discourse and record it, either on a voice recorder, your cell or utilizing a webcam or PC. Play it back and perceive how you do.

Focus on your talking propensities, what do you do that you wish you didn't, for example, perhaps you say "uh" or "mmm" to an extreme.

Observe what you need to right and afterward work on right it. Continue to do this with various points until you notice that the manner in which you talk is only the manner in which you believe that it should be.

The significant thing in this exercise is the manner by which you are talking, not the substance so, don't stress over what you are talking about, you are not being evaluated.

Activities to further develop composed relational abilities

The least difficult method for rehearsing your composed abilities is to keep a diary. Be that as it may, rather than a customary journal, which is casual, make this one a proper diary.

Focus on the punctuation and the substance.

In the event that you are serious areas of strength for not language structure and spelling, you should consider doing your diary on a word handling system and when it rectifies your punctuation and spelling focus on what you fouled up.

Continue to do this until you are done committing similar punctuation and spelling errors over and again.

Simply work out what happened that day, focusing on what matters and your responses to occasions, as they occurred.
At the point when we can impart actually, it makes our own and proficient lives better and more improved.

We limit the quantity of miscommunications and the quantity of misconception that can happen when wires get crossed or something is taken inappropriately or confounded, which can prompt contentions.

Anyone can just respond, yet it takes expertise to convey well, in any event, when in a conflict.

Correspondence is particularly significant in case of a conflict since it can assist with eliminating any confusion rapidly and resolve issues before them become more serious issues.

Figuring out how to convey is an expertise that albeit some are normally greater at it than others are, everyone can learn.

We as a whole can work on our capacity to impart.

Now that you view correspondence as more than simply talking, you are prepared to start developing your abilities and you will see a huge improvement over your own and proficient lives.

Correspondence is about the compromise of the discussion, about tuning in, recognizing, addressing, and replying.

It includes the manner in which we talk, how we say them, and what our non-verbal communication is the point at which we are conveying.

Now that you know about every one of the parts of correspondence, you know how to convey better since you will know about how you talk and of what your non-verbal communication is.

You will likewise be focusing on the non-verbal communication of individuals you converse with you and how they express things too, on the grounds that it passes on essential data too.

Mindfulness is half of the fight and practice is the other.

Printed in Great Britain
by Amazon